GOD
IS
YOUNG

MISERANDO ATQUE ELIGENDO

POPE FRANCIS

—

GOD
IS
YOUNG

—

A conversation with Thomas Leoncini

TRANSLATED FROM THE ITALIAN
BY ANNE MILANO APPEL

RANDOM HOUSE

NEW YORK

Published in the United States by Random House, an
imprint and division of Penguin Random House LLC,
New York.

RANDOM HOUSE and the HOUSE colophon are registered
trademarks of Penguin Random House LLC.

Originally published in Italian in Italy as *Dio é giovane* by
Piemme, an imprint of Mondadori Libri S.p.A., in 2018.

Hardback ISBN 9781984801401
Ebook ISBN 9781984801418

Printed in the United States of America on acid-free paper

randomhousebooks.com

246897531

FIRST EDITION

Book design by Simon M. Sullivan

For readers of all ages

FOR A REVOLUTION
OF TENDERNESS

We are taking no risks
when we make ourselves available to God,
and since His youth is unalterable,
our youth will be renewed
like that of the Church.

—MAURICE ZUNDEL

Youth, large, lusty, loving—
Youth full of grace, force, fascination,
Do you know that Old Age may come after you
with equal grace, force, fascination?

—WALT WHITMAN

"God is young; He is always new."

WE WERE SITTING across from each other in a room on the ground floor of the Domus Sanctae Marthae when Pope Francis spoke those words. I remember the exact moment perfectly: His eyes were alight with a spark, as if, along with the words, he wanted to communicate something profound and liberating at the same time. We were in the middle of our fifth meeting for this book, and that sentence struck me with unusual force: as if, for a moment, the story was leaving my hands—even as they meticulously recorded note after note—to go and shake a thousand other hands and reach a thousand other hearts.

With those memorable words, the pontiff was affirming that young people, or rather the great castoffs of our troubled times, are actually made "in the same mold" as God. That their best attributes are His. A

God who is not only Father—and Mother, as John Paul I earlier indicated—but also Son, and for that reason Brother. Francis was claiming a central place for these castoffs. He was delivering them from the margins and characterizing them as the protagonists of the present and of the future. Of a common history.

If it is true that young people are constantly subjected to a consumer society—overwhelmed by endless false starts that lead nowhere and constantly deluded by the promise of a social linearity that no longer exists—these pages spring from a desire to liberate them. The pontiff confirmed that the 2018 Synod on Young People is the ideal framework within which to understand and fully value their significance.

Francis has devoted much of his precious time to this project, and I have been merely the intermediary that the Pope chose to deliver his message, unfiltered, to young people throughout the world.

Young people are not the only castoffs of this consumer society; many adults are marginalized as well, especially the elderly, cut off by market-based logic and power principles.

It is necessary to find strength and determination, the pontiff says, but also tenderness, to create a bridge between young and old each and every day: Only by embracing the young and old can society truly be renewed, for the benefit of all who have been left behind and toward whom our gazes must constantly be directed.

Courage and wisdom are the essential ingredients of this much-needed "revolution of tenderness."

—T. L.

CONTENTS

GOD
IS
YOUNG

PART I

YOUNG PROPHETS
AND OLD DREAMERS

Pope Francis, I would like to start by asking you: What is youth?

———

YOUTH DOES NOT exist. When we talk about youth, we are often unconsciously referring to myths about youth. I like to think that youth does not exist, only young people. Just as old age does not exist, but old people do. And when I say "old" people I don't mean it as a bad word, on the contrary: It's a very beautiful word. We must be joyful and proud of being old, just as we are normally proud of being young. Old age is a privilege: It means having experience, being able to know and recognize our faults and our merits; it means the ability to be potentially renewed, just as when we were young; it means having acquired the understanding necessary to accept the past and, above all, to have learned from the past. Often we allow ourselves to be overwhelmed by the "culture of the adjective," without the substantiation of a noun. Youth, of course, is a noun, but it is a noun without any real substance; it is an idea that remains the orphan of a fanciful concept.

What do you see when you think of a young person?

═══

I SEE SOMEONE who is searching for his own path, who wants to fly on his two feet, who faces the world and looks out at the horizon with eyes full of the future, full of hope as well as illusions. A young person stands on two feet as adults do, but unlike the adults whose feet are parallel, he always has one foot forward, ready to set out, to spring ahead. Always racing onward. To talk about young people is to talk about promise and to talk about joy. Young people have so much strength; they are able to look ahead with hope. A young person is a promise of life that implies a certain degree of tenacity; he is foolish enough to delude himself and resilient enough to recover from that delusion.

Then, too, we can't talk about young people without touching on the theme of adolescence, because we must never underestimate that phase of life, which is probably the most difficult and the most important in a person's years. Adolescence marks the first true conscious contact with identity and represents a transitional phase not only in the child's life, but the life of the entire family. It is an intermediate phase, like a bridge that leads to the other side. And for this reason adolescents are neither here nor there, they are on their way, on the road, on the move. They are not children—nor do they want to be treated as such—but they are not adults, either. Yet they want to be treated as adults, especially when it comes to privileges. So we can probably say that adolescence is a state of inevitable tension, an introspective tension of the young. At the same time it is so intense that it is able to shake up the entire family, which is precisely what makes it so important. It is the young man's and the young woman's first revolution, the first life transformation, the transformation that changes one so much that it often upends friendships, loves, daily life as well. When we are adolescents the word "tomorrow" cannot be used with certainty. Even as adults we should be more cautious in uttering the word "tomorrow," particularly these days, but never are we as aware of the *moment* and the importance it holds than as adolescents. The moment, for the adolescent, is a world that can overturn his whole life. He thinks much more about the present during adolescence than during all the rest of his existence. Adolescents seek confrontation, they ask questions, they challenge everything, they look for answers. I can't stress enough how important it is to question everything. Adolescents are eager to learn, eager to fend for themselves and become independent. It is during this time that adults must be more understanding than ever and try to demonstrate the proper way through their actions, rather than insisting on teaching with words alone.

Young people go through different, even abrupt, states of mind, and their families with them. It is a phase that has its risks, undoubtedly, but above all it is a time of growth, for them and for their entire family.

Adolescence is not a pathology, and we cannot treat it as if it were. A child who experiences his adolescence positively—however difficult it may be for the parents—is a child with a future, with hope. I often worry about the current tendency to "medicate" our children at an early age. It seems we want to solve all our children's problems with medication, or by controlling their lives to "make the most of time," and so our children's agendas become busier than that of a high-level executive. I stress again: Adolescence is not a pathology that we must combat. It's part of normal, natural growth in our children's lives.

Where there is life there is movement, where there is movement there are changes, exploration, uncertainties, there is hope, there is joy, as well as anguish and misery.

What are the first images of your youth that come to mind? Try to picture yourself in Argentina when you were twenty . . .

═══

AT THAT AGE I was in the seminary. I had a very severe encounter with suffering: A piece of my lung was removed due to three cysts. This very intense experience colors my memory of the time you ask me to recall, but there is one very intimate thing I remember well: I was full of hopes and dreams.

Do you remember any of your dreams?

═══

I'LL TELL YOU an anecdote, so that you will understand the subtle gap between desires and reality. I was almost seventeen, I remember it was the day the musician Sergey Sergeyevich Prokofiev died. I loved his music very much. I was in the courtyard of my maternal grandmother's house, sitting at the table in the garden. I asked my grandmother: "How is it possible to be as brilliant as Prokofiev, to create the things he did?" And she replied: "Well, you see, Jorge, Prokofiev wasn't born that way; rather, he became that way. He struggled, worked hard, suffered, constructed: The beauty that you see today is the work of yesterday, of all that he suffered and went through in silence." I have never forgotten my conversations with my two grandmothers, figures whom I think of constantly and who are very important to me.

Have there been dreams that did not come true?

=====

OF COURSE, AND some I found frustrating. Like when I wanted to go to Japan to be a missionary but they wouldn't send me because of my lung operation. From a very young age, some people wrote me off, and yet I'm still here today, so it turned out all right . . . It's always best not to pay too much attention to those who wish us ill, don't you think?

Your calling from God came at a young age; do you recall the exact moment?

=====

THE STRONG CALLING from God occurred when I was nearly seventeen, on September 21, 1953, to be exact. I was on my way to meet my school friends for a day in the country. September 21 is the first day of spring in Argentina, and in those days there was an actual holiday dedicated to us young people. I was Catholic like my family, but prior to that day I had never thought of either the seminary or a future within the Church. Maybe as a child, when I was an altar boy, but it was a tenuous thing. Walking along, I saw the open door of the parish church and something drove me to go in. Inside I saw a priest coming toward me. I immediately felt a sudden desire to confess. I don't know what exactly happened during those moments, but whatever it was, it changed my life forever. I left the parish church and went home. I understood in a very strong, clear way what my life would be: I was to become a priest. In the meantime, I was studying chemistry, I started working in a test lab, I had a girlfriend, but inside me the idea of the priesthood continued to gain ever greater force.

So you were conflicted?

━━━

I KNEW WHAT my path would be, but some days I felt as if I were on a seesaw. I won't hide the fact that I, too, had my doubts, but God always wins, and after a while I found stability.

Have you ever felt betrayed by God?

━━━

NEVER. I WAS the one who betrayed Him. At times I even felt like God was turning away from me, just as I turned away from Him. At very dark moments you ask yourself, "Where are you, God?" I always believed that I was looking for God, but really it was He who was looking for me. He always gets there first and waits for us. I will use an expression that we use in Argentina: the Lord *primerea,* anticipates us, waits for us; we sin and He is waiting to forgive us. He is waiting to welcome us, to give us His love, and each time faith grows.

Why, when our society so badly needs young people, are young people cast aside?

———

NOT ONLY ARE young people discarded, but young people suffer greatly because they were born and raised in a society that has made the culture of discarding its supreme paradigm. In our throwaway society, "disposability" is routine: We use something once, knowing that when we're done, it will be thrown away. These attitudes run deep and take hold of people's habits and ways of thinking. Our society is too powerfully and compellingly dominated by an economic and financial crisis that does not revolve around men and women, but around the money and products created by men and women. We are in a phase of dehumanization of the human being: Not being able to work means not being able to have any dignity. We all know how different it feels to earn the bread that we bring home instead of receiving it from a charity . . .

Often young people are told—especially by affluent adults—not to think too much about money because it doesn't matter much, but today, in most cases, the money that a young person pursues is necessary for survival, to be able to look in the mirror with dignity, to be able to create a family, a future. And above all to be able to stop depending on his parents. What are your thoughts about this?

I THINK WE should ask young people for forgiveness because we don't always take them seriously. We don't always help them find their way or build the tools that could prevent them from being discarded. Often we don't know how to encourage their dreams, and we are unable to impassion them. It is normal to pursue money to create a family, a future, and to escape a subordinate role to adults, a role that young people today remain in for far too long. The important thing is not to feel a hunger for accumulation. There are people who live to accumulate money and think they have to accumulate it to live, as if money could be transformed into food for the soul. That means living as a slave to money, and we have learned that though money is tangible, there is something abstract, volatile, about it, something that can disappear overnight without warning: Think about the banking crisis and the recent defaults. I think what you're talking about, however, is an important issue: You mentioned money in relation to the need for livelihood and therefore work. I can tell you that it is work that feeds the soul, work that can be transformed into *joie de vivre,* into collaboration, into unified intent and teamwork. Not money. And there must be work for everyone. Every human being must have a chance to work, to demonstrate to himself and to his loved ones that he can earn a living. We cannot accept exploitation; we must not accept the fact that many young people are exploited by employers, with false promises, with payments that never come, with the excuse that they are young and must gain experience. We cannot accept having employers demand temporary and even unpaid work from young people, as often happens. I know that there are cases where they are asked to work for nothing, sometimes even requiring prequalification to be able to do so. This is exploitation and produces the most abysmal feelings in the soul, feelings that steadily grow and can even change a young person's personality.

Young people ask to be heard, and we have a duty to listen to them and to accept them, to not exploit them. There are no excuses for that.

Let's consider a talented young man, not a "rich daddy's boy," but someone with a great desire to achieve, someone with zero contacts, zero corruption, and zero desire to enter into any arrangements of dependence. What can he actually do to keep from being relegated to the role of castoff? Is the so-called brain drain really the only way to escape this machinery and construct a clean future for himself? I say this because for many young people escape is the only possible salvation still imaginable . . .

———

MY ANSWER TO you is one word: *parrhesia*. I speak of it as courage, as being fervent in our actions. In prayer, for example, I also advise young people to pray with *parrhesia*. Which means that we should never be content with asking once, twice, three times. We must believe, ask, and pray for something as long as we can. That was how David prayed when he pleaded for his dying son (2 Samuel 12:15–18). It is essential to stay the course, as Moses did when he prayed for the rebellious people. He never changed sides, he did not bargain, he never stopped believing and believing in them. Let's not ever forget this concept: Intercession is not for wimps. In the Gospel Jesus speaks to us clearly: "Ask and it will be given to you; seek and you will find; knock and the door will be opened to you" (Matthew 7:7). And since Jesus was eager to make us clearly understand, He gave us the example of the man who rings his neighbor's doorbell late one night to ask him for three loaves of bread; unconcerned about being considered ill-mannered, he simply wants to obtain food for his guest (Luke 11:5–8). For such perseverance and constancy in prayer, Jesus promises the certainty of success: "For everyone who asks, receives; and the one who seeks, finds; and to the one who knocks, the door will be opened" (Matthew 7:8). Jesus also explains the reason for succeeding: "Which one of you would hand his son a stone when he asks for a loaf of bread, or a snake when he asks for a fish? If you then, who are wicked, know how to give good gifts to your children, how much more will your heavenly Father give good things to those who ask Him" (Matthew 7:9–11).

Courage must never be confused with recklessness; on the contrary, recklessness is the bitter enemy of courage. But those who lack courage remain *apocado* ("timid"), as they say in Spanish: They say *apocado* when talking about someone who never takes one step in life for fear of slipping.

What governs *parrhesia* is the ability to wait patiently (in Greek, *hypomone*) when facing difficulties. *Parrhesia* always goes together with *hypomone;* even in prayer we struggle with courage and patience, each and every day.

How can young people feel they are at the center of things, when instead they are routinely discarded?

BY MAKING THEM into protagonists, or better yet *allowing* them to become protagonists. To understand a young person today you have to understand him in motion, you can't sit still and claim to be on his wavelength. If we want to talk with a young person we must be in motion, too, and then it will be he who slows down to listen to us; he will be the one to decide to do it. And when he slows down a different tempo will be established: a stride in which the young will begin to set a slower pace in order to be heard and the elderly will speed up to find a common meeting ground. They will both make an effort: the young ones to go more slowly and the old ones to move faster. This could be a mark of progress. I would like to quote Aristotle, who in his *Rhetoric* (II, 12:2) says: "... youth has a long future before it and a short past behind it: on the first day of one's life one has nothing at all to remember, and can only look forward. They are easily cheated, owing to the sanguine disposition just mentioned. Their hot tempers and hopeful dispositions make them more courageous than older men are; the hot temper prevents fear, and the hopeful disposition creates confidence; we cannot feel fear so long as we are feeling angry, and any expectation of good makes us confident ... [And] they have exalted notions."

Starting with those born in the eighties, which I call "the liquid generation," the relationship between young people and religious faith has taken a different turn with respect to the past: There are more and more young people who grow up without a strong family religious tradition. What do you think this can be attributed to? Can this prospect change?

———

TO THE DEVELOPMENT of secularization itself, but also to the general crises of families and the economy. I am also strongly convinced of the importance of sobriety in the life of the Church: The men and women of the Church should *clothe themselves* only in that which can serve the practice of faith and compassion for God's people and *strip themselves* of what is superfluous. It is always better to have empty pockets, because the Devil persistently lives in full pockets; in fact, if he enters our lives, he comes through the pockets.

In a society that seems to be swarming with double-dealers and ravenous wolves, how can we convince young people that they can meet individuals along the way who live by God's principles?

———

THE ANSWER IS: thanks to other young people. Because a young person has something of the prophet about him, and he must be aware of it. He must be conscious of having the wings of a prophet, the ways of a prophet, the ability to prophesy, to *say* but also to *do*. A prophet in our time has the power to condemn, certainly, but also to see what's ahead. Young people have both of these qualities. They are able to condemn, even though they do not always express their condemnation well. And they also have the ability to scan the future and see farther ahead. But adults are often cruel and ignore the strength that young people have. Adults often uproot young people; instead of helping them to be prophets for the good of society, they pull up their roots and turn them into orphans and castoffs. Today's young people are growing up in an uprooted society.

What do you mean by "uprooted society"?

I MEAN A society made up of individuals, families, who are gradually losing their connections, that vital fabric so important for us to feel part of one another, engaged in a common pursuit with others—"common" in the broadest sense of the word. A society is rooted if it is aware of belonging to a history and to other people, in the noblest sense of the term. It is uprooted, on the other hand, if the young grow up in families without a history, without a memory, and therefore without roots. We've all known since we were children how important roots are, physically even: If there are no roots, any wind ends up blowing you away. For this reason one of the first things we must think about as parents, as families, as pastors is a course of action whereby roots can be put down, where bonds can be generated, and where the vital connections that allow us to feel *at home* can be cultivated. For an individual to know that he has no roots, that he does not belong to anyone, is a terrible feeling of alienation: There is nothing worse than feeling like a stranger in your own home, without a kernel of identity to share with other human beings. Roots make us less alone and more complete.

Today social networks would seem to offer an opportunity to connect with others; the Web makes young people feel part of a distinct group. But the problem with the Internet is its virtual nature: It leaves young people *up in the air* and thus it is extremely volatile. I like to recall a quote from the Argentinian poet Francisco Luis Bernárdez: *"Por lo que el árbol tiene de florido, vive de lo que tiene sepultado."* ("What the tree has visibly in bloom, thrives on what is buried beneath.")

How can we guard against an uprooted society?

I THINK A powerful way to guard against it is through dialogue: a dialogue between the young and the elderly, an interaction between young and old, even temporarily bypassing adults. Young and old must talk to one another, and they must do it more often: This is extremely important! And the elderly as well as the young must seize the initiative. There is a passage from the Bible (Joel 3:1) which says: ". . . your old men will dream dreams, your young men will see visions."

But our society discards both the one and the other, it discards the young as well as the old. Yet the salvation of the old is to pass memory on to the young, which makes the old true dreamers of the future; whereas the salvation of the young is to accept these teachings, these dreams, and carry them into the future, like prophets. In order for our young people to have visions, to be *dreamers* themselves, and to be able to face the future boldly and courageously, they must listen to the prophetic dreams of their forefathers. Old dreamers and young prophets are our uprooted society's path to salvation: Two generations of discarded throwaways can save us all.

All of this is related to what I call the revolution of tenderness, because for a young person to approach an old person requires tenderness, and it takes tenderness for an elderly individual to approach a young person. The message must originate from both sides; there are no hierarchies, each must seek the other out.

By contrast, however, and unfortunately, I always see a great deal of competition among adults—this time I am not speaking about the elderly, but about the generation in between—and young people; this competition is directed by adults toward young people, and even toward the very young. In many cases one might even speak of rivalries.

How did this rivalry come about?

IT SEEMS THAT growing up, aging, *maturing,* is bad. It is synonymous with a used-up, dissatisfied life. Today it seems that everything hides behind makeup and a mask. As if the very fact of living did not make sense. Recently I talked about how sad it is for someone to want to have a *face-lift* of the heart! How sorrowful it is that someone would want to erase the wrinkles of the many encounters, the many joys and sorrows! Too often there are adults who play at being youthful, who feel the need to put themselves on the level of an adolescent, unable to see that it is a deception. It's a trick of the Devil. I can't understand how it is possible for an adult to feel in competition with a young child, but unfortunately it happens more and more frequently. It's as if the adults were saying: "You are young, you have this great potential and this enormous promise, but I want to be younger than you, and I can be, I can pretend to be that and be better at it than you are."

There are too many parents who in their minds are adolescents, who play at an "eternally ephemeral" life and, consciously or not, make their children victims of this perverse game. Because they raise children who, on the one hand, start off in a culture of the ephemeral and, on the other hand, grow up more and more uprooted, in a society that I call just that: "uprooted."

Some years ago, in Buenos Aires, I took a taxi: The driver was very worried, nearly disconsolate. He immediately struck me as a troubled man. He looked at me in the rearview mirror and said, "Are you the cardinal?" I answered yes and he replied: "What should we do about these young people? I don't know how to manage my children anymore. Last Saturday four girls came over, barely of age, my daughter's age, and they had four bags full of bottles. I asked what they were going to do with all that vodka, whiskey, and other stuff; their response was: 'We're going home to get ready for tonight's *movida*.'" I think deeply and often about this story: Those girls were like orphans, they seemed rootless, they wanted to become orphans of their bodies and their reason. To ensure a fun evening they had to get there already drunk. But what does it mean to get to the *movida* already drunk?

It means arriving there full of illusions and bringing with you a body that is not in your control, a body that does not respond to the head or the heart, a body that responds only to instincts, a body without memory, a body composed only of ephemeral flesh. We are nothing without the head and without the heart; we are nothing if we act in the grip of instinct, without reason. Our heads and our hearts bring us closer together in a real way; and they bring us closer to God so that we can think about God and can decide to go and seek Him. Using our reason and our hearts we can also understand someone who is troubled, we can put ourselves in his place, we can become agents for good, we can instill altruism. Let us never forget the words of Jesus: ". . . whoever wishes to be great among you will be your servant; whoever wishes to be first among you will be the slave of all. For the Son of Man did not come to be served but to serve . . ." (Mark 10:43–45).

And should those who govern think of these words of Jesus?

=====

TO GOVERN IS to serve each of us, each of our brethren who make up humanity, without forgetting anyone. A person who governs must learn to look up to talk to God but not to act like God. And he must look down to lift up those who have fallen.

Man's gaze must always be turned in those two directions. Look up to God and down to those who have fallen if you want to become great: The answers to the most difficult questions are always found by looking in those two directions at the same time.

What advice can you give to those who govern?

=====

NOT TO LISTEN solely to intermediaries, but to lower themselves, to actually look around. I advise those who govern to *touch* reality. And to stay away from vanity and pride: A vain, proud man does not know wisdom, and a man without wisdom always ends badly.

What is the worst consequence of sin that can be committed by those in power?

———

DEFINITELY ONE'S OWN self-destruction. But there is another consequence, and though I don't know if it is really the worst, it occurs very frequently: that is, to end up being ridiculous. And you can't come back from being ridiculous.

Who was one of the most ridiculous figures in history? If you ask me, Pontius Pilate: If he had known that he was dealing with the Son of God, and that the Son of God had used His power to wash the feet of His disciples, would he have washed his hands of Him? I really don't think so!

The evangelist John tells us that the Lord was aware of having all the power of the world in His hands. And what did He decide to do with all that power? A single act, which was an act of service, specifically the service of forgiveness. Jesus decided that from that moment on power should be transformed, forever, into service. What was the true prophetic message of all this? He deposed the powerful from their thrones and lifted up the humble. Power is service and must enable others to feel well cared for, according to their dignity. The one who serves is the equal of the one who is served.

So then, in practical terms, what should someone who has a lot of power do?

THE MORE POWER one has, the more one must be willing to serve. Those with a little more power must be willing to serve a little more. This is where there should be real competition: among those who want to serve more.

To answer your question more fully, however, I can tell you about fifteen very dangerous diseases for men: I wrote them as a guide for the Curia, but they are equally useful for those in power and for each of us. I would say that in some way they are actually linked to power.

The first is the disease of feeling you are immortal or downright indispensable: It derives from narcissism and is typical of those who passionately gaze at their own image while failing to see God in the faces of others; worst of all, they fail to recognize the Light of Jesus in the eyes of those most in need. The medicine to cure it is the grace to know that we are ourselves sinners and to say with all our hearts: "We are unprofitable servants; we have done what we were obliged to do" (Luke 17:10).

The second is the disease that I call "marthaism" (based on Martha of Bethany, recounted in the Gospel of Luke), namely excessive activity: It afflicts those who immerse themselves in work, inevitably neglecting to sit at the feet of Jesus (Luke 10:38–42). Neglecting needed rest leads to stress, anxiety, and useless agitation.

The third disease is that of mental and emotional petrification, typical of those who have a heart of stone and a "hard head" (Acts 7:51). It is the disease of those who, as they get ahead, lose their serenity, their vivacity and audacity, and end up becoming paper pushers. It typifies those who lose the desire to compete, who lose the will to wake up every morning and go on living as if they were just starting out.

The fourth disease is that of too much planning and productivity: When a person plans everything out minutely and believes that by having a perfect plan things will progress solely for that reason, he becomes a bookkeeper, an accountant of existence. In fact, one cannot confine the freedom of the Holy Spirit in a plan. The Holy Spirit brings freshness, imagination, innovation—notice the similarity to the concept of youth that we talked about.

The fifth disease is that of dissociation: It is as if the foot said to the arm, "I don't need you," or the hand said to the head, "I'm in charge," causing uneasiness and indignation.

The sixth disease is what I call "spiritual Alzheimer's": It is forgetting one's own path to salvation, one's personal romance with the Lord, the "love you had at first" (Revelation 2:4), one's own roots; it happens in particular to those who live hedonistically, to those who are slaves to their passions, their whims, their manias, their phobias, their instincts, at times the lowest and most squalid.

The seventh disease is that of rivalry and vainglory: It can be seen when appearances, the cut of one's clothes and badges of honor, become the primary objective in life, forgetting the words of Saint Paul: "Do nothing out of selfishness or out of vainglory; rather, humbly regard others as more important than yourselves, each looking out not for his own interests, but [also] everyone for those of others" (Philippians 2:3–4).

The eighth disease is that of existential schizophrenia. It is typical of those who live a double life; it is the fruit of the hypocrisy of mediocrity and of the progressive emotional emptiness that degrees, honors, or titles cannot fill. It is the disease of those who lose touch with reality, with actual people, and become simple administrators of bureaucratic matters. These people create their own parallel world where they set aside everything they sternly teach others and begin to live a hidden and often dissolute life.

The ninth disease is that of gossiping, whispering,

and spreading rumors. It is a serious disease that often starts out simply, maybe as just talk, and then takes hold of the person, turning him into a "sower of discord," like Satan, and in many cases a cold-blooded murderer of another person's reputation. Yes, because a person can also be killed by language, and one must never underestimate the power of words. One can speak of a "terrorism of gossip," because the spreading of rumors truly resembles the action of a terrorist: dropping the bomb with his words, he destroys others, then leaves calmly as if nothing had happened.

The tenth disease is that of deifying leaders. It is the disease of those who fawn over individuals in power, hoping to obtain their favor. Never fall victim to careerism and opportunism; we must honor God and always think about what we should *give,* rather than about what we can *get.*

The eleventh disease is that of indifference toward others: It is when each individual thinks only of himself and loses the sincerity and warmth of human relationships. But it also occurs when the more experienced person does not put his knowledge at the service of less experienced colleagues. Or when, out of jealousy or guile, one is happy to see the other person fall instead of helping him up and encouraging him.

The twelfth disease is that of the glum face, that is,

the face worn by grim, dour individuals, who think that to be serious you need to wear a forbidding, stern expression and treat others, especially those you consider your subordinates, with rigor, severity, and arrogance.

The thirteenth disease is that of "consuming consumption," of consumerism. It is the disease of accumulation: when the individual tries to fill an existential void in his heart by accumulating material goods, not out of need, but only to feel secure. In reality, no material possessions can be taken with us because "the shroud has no pockets." Have you ever seen a moving truck accompany a funeral procession? I haven't . . .

The fourteenth disease is that of closed circles, where belonging to the clique becomes even more important than belonging to Christ. This disease almost always begins with good intentions, but as time goes by it results in harmful practices, enslaving the members.

The last disease I want to talk about is that of worldly gain and exhibitionism, when the individual transforms his service into power and his power into possessions in order to acquire material gain or still more power. It is the disease of power that feeds on itself, of people who insatiably strive to increase their powers and who, to achieve that goal, are capable of vilifying, slandering, and discrediting others, even in newspapers and magazines. It is a disease that is proudly nurtured by vanity. The Desert Fathers compared vanity to an onion because—they said—it is difficult to reach its core: You continue peeling it, but there is always something left; at the very least the odor remains. Vanity is a soap bubble, being vain is hiding behind a mask.

Are there some moral diseases of man that are worse than others?

THERE IS AN extremely serious disease which I am very concerned about and which is quite widespread, especially in this day and age: the inability to feel guilty.

I worry about those I have called "ambitious climbers" who, behind their international degrees and their technical language (so often "gaseous"), may be concealing a precarious wisdom but most of all conceal an almost total lack of humanity. Not infrequently, many people, afraid of suffering and struggle, of hard work and sacrifice, prefer to believe these individuals, who, though unreliable, are often endorsed. But what would human beings be without suffering?

Here I've touched on another theme which I think is very important: the fear of moral suffering. It is by suffering that we learn to grow day by day. Suffering and life's trials provide us with an indispensable opportunity to look deeply into our souls and to understand our limitations, so that we can ask ourselves: Is it really still necessary for more blood to be shed in order for our wounded, futile pride to recognize its defeat?

Suffering can also teach us a useful lesson, let's not forget: Suffering can help us understand how far down we are delving and thus be instrumental in radically changing our attitudes, our behaviors. To be clear, this should not be confused with masochism. I'm talking about suffering that is not sought, but that comes and must therefore be faced.

I would like to go back to young people's dissatisfaction: Can the fact that the young never find fulfillment be closely linked to their fear of getting old? What I mean is: Is it possible they want to stay young forever so as not to see the hope for opportunity come to an end? It would be in line with data indicating that more and more young and very young people are resorting to plastic surgery . . .

To sum things up, there are adults who, as you say, are forever chasing the myth of eternal youth and young people who have the same fear of growing old as the adults do . . .

What do you think about the prevalence of plastic surgery among young people?

═══

I THINK THAT young people, both male and female, increasingly resort to plastic surgery mainly to conform to society's standards and so they won't end up being discarded; at least they try to prolong the illusion of being protagonists. Unfortunately, until we get over this throwaway culture, the most fragile individuals will continue to delude themselves that a solution can be found in the ephemeral.

We must all realize that a society built on the ephemeral and on discarding creates only momentary and illusory pleasures and not deep and lasting joys.

Among the current trends of the ephemeral, which concern you the most?

═══

WHAT MAKES ME reflect a lot, and also frightens me, is the proliferation of what in Argentina are called *mascotas,* "mascots"—those little pets that people increasingly carry around with them, all day every day. Sometimes there is a strong love for the animals, and this is an important factor that in my opinion must be taken into consideration, because God created man but also animals and the environment. But it worries me when people—gripped by a troubling sense of loneliness and perhaps by a desire to experience what it's like to "play God"—become completely absorbed in their rapport with the *mascotas*. They use the animals and do not respect their dignity. It is an illusory way of creating an object of affection: a contrived friendship, a convenient family, a handy loved one. It is a loved one in one's own image and likeness, bypassing human beings and social relationships, viewing the "mascot" as a person. In reality, this animal becomes a slave of its owner, and the latter delights in a relationship created perhaps to replace human social relations, which by contrast require dialogue and mutual give-and-take. The relationship with the "mascot" is likely to become a binding, one-way relationship, in which one is always forgiven no matter what and where one can do anything. All this has nothing to do with love for animals, which is noble and therefore entirely different.

Then, too, I am certainly very concerned about the cosmetic and plastic surgery industry. We cannot afford to have them become a necessity; for the good of us all, we cannot accept the spread of an artificial aesthetic. All this depersonalizes man's beauty, making him look "the same as everyone else."

Don't we realize how awful it is to become "the same as everyone"?

Why would anyone want to look like the norm?

Why don't we love each other the way God made us?

Why is the human being, male and female, increasingly becoming a slave to appearance and to acquiring possessions, and forgetting how essential it is to *be*?

These are questions that I think of often, because I find these topics crucial in a society that is as liquid and full of inconclusive beginnings as ours is. Inconclusive beginnings: That is perhaps a fitting image.

Related to that, you just have to log on to Facebook, Instagram, Twitter, or Pinterest and type "#lips #kisses" to witness a profuse ode to plastic surgery, for both young men and young women. The more work they've had done, the more "likes" they get. What do you think of all this?

═══

I FIND IT worrying, because here, too, we are trying to play God: attempting to create an image different from the one you have from nature, from natural history. The constant construction of a new, parallel existence is likely to lead to dependence and end up replacing what God has given us. Because life is a gift, I never get tired of it. If I receive a gift and continue altering it to my taste, every day, how can the one who gave it to me not be disappointed?

God forgives, that's true, but we should reflect more on what we really are, on our essence. Though more and more I realize that the cause of all this is society itself, which consumes and consumes and consumes, leaving little room for the essential and focusing a great deal on appearance. And therefore "redoing" oneself becomes a necessity, to prevent being tossed aside.

Taking proper care of oneself, on the other hand, is quite another thing—wanting to make a good impression on others, self-respect, decorum, a positive appreciation of oneself, are the result of a fitting self-esteem and a sense of one's own dignity. This is the right and proper care of the body and of one's image, which expresses care and inner beauty outwardly as well. This is a good and proper thing.

Balance is difficult, I know. It is difficult to change a human being without changing the society that nurtures him, and this is where I want to return to my firm confidence in the young, who along with the old can change society.

Can you tell me about a personal experience of yours regarding an effective relationship between young and old?

═══

I'LL START FROM the beginning: When we were children, at two o'clock in the afternoon every Saturday, my mother made us listen to the opera that was broadcast on Radio Nacional (we did not yet have a record player) and, as a true lover of music, she explained to us the stories of those melodies and their creators. Thanks to these very early experiences, I became ardently interested in culture and in the joy of creativity. Later, as a young man, Saturday remained a very important day for me, because I could go to the opera house and see the performances live. I remember perfectly my seat at the theater, the one in the section that in Argentina we call the *gallinero* ("chicken roost"): I sat there because I paid less. Next door to our house in Buenos Aires there was a family, and a widow with two children lived with them, too. She was the family's housekeeper, but had great dignity; she was an extremely cultured woman, who really loved reading philosophy books. She also had a certain amount of authority: She was the person the family relied on to run the house, and everyone trusted her. She and I talked frequently, and I vividly remember the first time I invited her to see the opera with me. She was happy: During the performance I looked at her and saw her smile. This made me feel good, I had treated her "invisibility" with consideration. I had ministered to her, but she, at the same time, had ministered to my soul because she made me feel good; I was proud to go with her on a Saturday to see the opera. When we left the theater we discussed the performance, we exchanged criticisms and opinions. These experiences were so intense and delightful that I still remember them as if they took place this morning. This made me grow, it enabled me to commune for the first time with an elderly woman who was not part of my biological family, and that is very important.

And here I come back to how a young person can be helpful to an older person and an elderly person to a young one. To continue answering your question, I would like to talk about another individual. I always carry a medal of the Sacred Heart that was given to me by a Sicilian woman who helped my mother two days a week, a widow who worked as a domestic to provide for her children. After I entered the seminary, I didn't see her again for about twenty years. Then one day, I think it was in 1981, when I was rector at the Collegio Massimo, she came to the school to look for me: They told me she was there, but I was very busy with the day's problems, with various claims on my attention, and I told the secretary to tell her that I was away at the time.

You can't imagine how I wept when I realized what I had done: years of weeping and guilt.

I prayed that I would find her again and that the Lord would forgive my wrong.

One day when I was a bishop, a priest told me that he had stopped to talk to the driver of a taxi, a man who said he knew me. He gave this priest his phone number, asking him if he could please pass it on to me. He was the woman's son! I finally saw the chance to atone for what for me had been a great sin, which had made me suffer a great deal. Right away I called the man, who told me that his mother was still alive, and I immediately asked to see her again. That woman had been very important to me, she had taught me about the cruelty of war, she had told me all about that period in history, which I'd been able to see through her eyes. After we were reunited, I never stopped thanking the Lord for this favor He'd granted me. Then, when she was ninety-two, I was with her at the moment of death.

Those who have experience have a duty to make it available to young people, selflessly.

Is God for everyone? Even for those who do not believe in God?

=====

WHEN I WAS in Krakow for World Youth Day, a young university student asked me: "How can I talk with an atheist who is my age? What can I say to a young atheist who has no relationship with God?"

I replied: "Why do you feel the need to talk? We should always *do,* not *say.* Just *do.* If you start talking, you'll be proselytizing and proselytizing means using people. Young people are very sensitive to verbal testimonies, they need men and women who are examples, who do without demanding anything from others, who show themselves for what they are. The other young person will be the one to ask you questions, and that will be the time to talk."

So are we all God's children?

=====

GOD HAS GIVEN birth to all of us, without distinction. God is also our mother. Pope John Paul I, too, upheld the image of God as the mother of humanity. Think about this passage from the prophet Isaiah (49:14–15): "But Zion said, 'The Lord has forsaken me; my Lord has forgotten me.' Can a mother forget her infant, be without tenderness for the child of her womb?"

Feelings of tenderness are very common in the Scriptures, the love of God is also "visceral," to put it in human terms. I find the passage of Luke 13:34 very significant, which says: "Jerusalem, Jerusalem, you who kill the prophets and stone those sent to you, how many times I yearned to gather your children together as a hen gathers her brood under her wings, but you were unwilling!" When Jesus spoke those words He wept over Jerusalem . . .

But I would like to add something more about God. In the book of the Apocalypse (Revelation 21:5) there is this phrase: "The one who sat on the throne said, 'Behold, I make all things new.'" God therefore is He who always renews, because He is always new: God is young! God is the Eternal One who has no time, but is able to renew and rejuvenate Himself and all things continually. The most distinctive attributes of the young are also His. He is young because He "makes all things new" and loves innovation; because He astonishes and loves astonishment; because He dreams and wants us to dream; because He is strong and enthusiastic; because He forms relationships and asks us to do the same: He is social.

I think of the image of a young person and I see that he, too, has the potential to be "eternal," drawing upon his purity, his creativity, his courage, and his energy, along with the dreams and wisdom of the old. It is a cycle that comes full circle, that creates a new continuity and reminds me of the image of eternity.

The sociologist Erich Fromm spoke of cybernetic religion: Man has made himself a god, having acquired the capability for a second creation of the world that would replace the first creation by God.

Transferring Fromm's thinking to today, and even more so to the very near future, we have made computers and the Internet into new gods, and we have deluded ourselves into thinking that we are like God by using them.

Human beings, despite being effectively powerless, manage to think they are omnipotent with the support of the Internet and computers. Not only that: If we add plastic surgery, the reconstruction of man by man himself, and the pets you mentioned as an example of formulated, ready-made affection, aren't we talking about a humanity that is deluding itself, as never before in history, where its omnipotence is concerned?

═══

ONE COULD CERTAINLY say that. Though technology is more good than bad. It is appropriate to be happy about the great strides made by technology and science, which have become increasingly interconnected. All in all the last two centuries have brought about continuous, ever more important changes: We went from the steam engine to the telegraph to electricity, the automobile, the airplane, chemical industries, information technology, and most recently the digital revolution, robotics, biotechnologies, and nanotechnologies. All of these changes have certainly been great steps forward for humanity. But let's ask ourselves a question: How did man create all these things? The answer lies in a single word: "creativity." I would like to quote John Paul II, who in 1981 said: "Science and technology are wonderful products of a God-given human creativity which is a gift from God." When we talk about technology we must always remember that, in its infinite aspects, it has meant real progress, a remedy for numerous ills that affect the human being.

At the same time it is also true that all of these technologies have given man enormous power; in particular it is important to consider how those who have substantial economic prospects can exploit and control those technologies to a staggering degree. Here I agree with you when you say that humanity has never before had so much power over itself. Unfortunately, the question I often ask myself is this: Is humanity using all that power well? Having started the sentence with "unfortunately," I don't think I need to add anything more . . .

How can a young person find fulfillment without becoming part of the machinery of corruption? To quote you: The difference between sinners and corrupt individuals is that the former recognize the sin as such and wrestle with it humbly; the latter systematically elevate their way of life and sin without regretting it.

———

CORRUPT INDIVIDUALS ARE the order of the day. But young people must not accept corruption as if it were any other sin, they must never grow used to corruption, because what we let slide by today will reoccur tomorrow, until we adapt to it and become an indispensable cog in its wheel. Young people have purity, as do the elderly, and together, young and old must take pride in coming together—clean, pure, sound—to outline a common path of life without corruption. I want to be clear in explaining the idea of purity as a concept that unites young and old. Young people are pure because they have not personally experienced corruption. They are to a certain extent malleable, and this can also prove to be dangerous because the purity they have can turn into something ugly, impure, dirty, especially if they have to cope with repeated attempts at proselytism and mass conformity. With old age—speaking in general terms, because unfortunately not every specific case is like this—human beings return in a certain sense to a "pure" state, they no longer have the hunger for success, for power, they are no longer influenced by the ephemeral as they may have been as adults. And then, too: Even an old penitent, who years before had been involved in corruption, can be useful to a young person's growth. Such an old man is, in fact, familiar with the mechanisms of corruption and can recognize them; he can show the young man how to sidestep them, by sharing his experience, and explaining how to avoid ending up like him. But let's return to the importance of verbal testimony.

The corrupt individual does not know humility, he always manages to say, "It wasn't me," and he does so with the face of a hypocritical little angel—"*fa la mugna quàcia*," as we say in Piedmontese dialect.* He lives a fraudulent life, gets tired of seeking forgiveness, and very soon stops asking for it. In contrast, let's think of the Gospels: Matthew, the good thief, and Zacchaeus are all figures who sin, but they are not corrupt, they have not yielded to corruption; a lifeline was left to them to save them from corruption.

---

* The expression in Piedmontese dialect—"*fa la mugna quàcia*"—literally means to act like a pious nun: "*mugna*" means "monaca" or nun, and "*quàcia*" means "quatto," bowed over. It is used to refer to someone who seems like a little saint, fakes humility, and pretends to be a holy innocent.

A chink of hope in the heart is enough to let God in.

Much has already been taken from the young, but there is hope as long as they are not corrupted.

What, in your opinion, could be the mission of every young person to help other young people find a place in this society?

———

YOUNG PEOPLE MUST regard one another as one big family. And those who are able to emerge, to find their way, must feel responsible for sending a message, must act like prophets, in order to tell others how to do good, to do good things. Those who are up ahead must help others to be strong.

What can be done to raise awareness about the social emergency that we are experiencing?

———

WE'VE TALKED ABOUT a "slap in the face"; I mean a cultural slap, obviously, not a physical one. We must be able to demonstrate with both acts and testimony that a dialogue between old and young can enrich everyone and bring about an evolution of society. That would be a great cultural slap. I even saw an example of this in its own small way: All it took was to arrange for a group of young people to visit a nursing home for the elderly. It was a wonderful experience for everyone. Now, with the proper scale, just imagine what would happen if in daily life a real synergy between young and old were created.

You are truly able to make young people all over the world feel understood—believers, agnostics or atheists, heterosexuals and homosexuals—and you do this through your actions: You understand the fragility of the young and you help them, you talk to them about it, you urge them to accept themselves, you don't claim to teach, but with your purity you teach a great deal more than any self-proclaimed teacher. And the purity is immediate, it has no need of shortcuts or explanations.

What would you think if I tell you that your papacy is an ode to fragility and to those who are discarded?

I WOULD SAY just one thing . . . I wish that it were so. I am a believer, and I am amazed by God's fragility in Jesus, at Jesus "the castoff."

PART II

IN THIS WORLD

Climate change is increasingly alarming. In your opinion, do young people recognize the urgency of the matter? Are young people today more likely to protect the ecosystem than previous generations?

＝＝＝＝

THIS IS A subject that is very close to my heart, because only by protecting the ecosystem can we protect our children, our grandchildren, and every future generation. Consequently, caring for the environment should be written in red ink and highlighted on the first page of every political agenda. And this is related to another consideration, which is all too frightening: the submission of politics to all other sectors, such as finance; a politics of "consuming consumption" is a politics that ends up being invisible, because it inevitably consumes itself as well.

But you asked me if young people today are more alert to climate problems and to the environment in general, and my answer is yes. Not just because I have great confidence in young people, but because they have many more means of becoming aware of the gravity of the situation than past generations did. The Internet is a "blessing" in this regard: It enables young people's awareness to be raised through other young people and allows people in disadvantaged conditions to communicate. We must constantly consider those who are less fortunate, those who don't interest the corrupt and who instead can be transformed from forgotten castoffs to "bearers of joy."

What connection do you see between raising awareness of the climate and discarding those who are most vulnerable?

———

I SEE THEM as very closely related, because we are talking about the same logic: The logic that feels no particular concern for the environment is the same logic that discards the most vulnerable, that does not include them. This happens because the logic I'm talking about does not think it makes sense to invest so that the weakest, those who start out in life with a handicap, can get ahead. I strongly believe that good politics should think big, should have a very broad vision that does not exclude the weakest and that does not spend governmental time on interminable and sometimes insubstantial discussions. It is necessary to act quickly, thinking especially of those who have been left behind and not just about those who are ahead, as many people like to do. The reason that young people discredit politics—though they're not the only ones—is solely the fault of government's ineffective public policies and its excessive, all too visible corruption. The shame associated with sinning seems to be lacking, and that in itself is a terrible sin.

Is the environmental crisis due more to politics or to the economy?

═══

IF POLITICS THINKS only of preserving and increasing its power and the economy is solely concerned with immediate utility, a double admission of guilt is probably needed, and above all a synergy that would help solve the problem at its root. But if these two principles dominate, is there any possibility of preserving the environment and looking after the weakest?

I would like to say something about the economy, however, and I think this is the right opportunity: I don't want to demonize the market as a way of structuring our trade. Nevertheless, we have to ask ourselves a specific question: What does the very idea of "market" call to mind? People buying and selling. Anything that is not part of buying and selling has no place. And what if we think about the fact that not everything is sold and not everything can be bought? Spirituality, love, friendship: None of these can be bought, yet it seems that in order to "be someone" you have to *possess* something rather than *be* something. I am likewise referring to the acquisition of executive or managerial positions: These are all *things*. You feel like you are someone because of that position, which gives you a role, assigns a title to your name, so you are no longer ashamed of who you are, whatever your origin, because you have acquired that role at the banquet of consumption. Those who partake of the banquet of consumption are assured of a little more security so they won't end up among the discarded. It's like having a little battery power still left on your cellphone. You know, young people today are terrified of being left with a dead battery in their smartphones: It means being *out of touch* with the world, excluded from connections, from the "possibilities" of the banquet of consumption. And when you are excluded someone else can "steal" from you what you might have bought. The higher the position, the more imposing the name on the business card, the more the battery seems fully charged. But those who live exclusively in the consumer society will always have an hour-by-hour independence. Something that cannot be bought, on the other hand, is much more valuable because it is personal, ours alone, nobody can steal it from us with money. That which cannot be bought, like love, affection, friendship, esteem, must be carefully cultivated, must be tended with extreme care, and we must pour our hearts into it to keep it from wilting. We must water it with our hearts. The danger of these worthy gifts is not theft or being left with a dead battery: The real danger is to let them wilt because of our lack of care.

The media deals with the issue of nuclear threat practically every day, in particular with the dangers of the North Korean regime. I am reminded of Fromm, who spoke of modern man at the service of the "goddess of destruction," therefore at the service of his own creation. The nuclear threat is no longer cited as a threat to man, but as a threat in itself: In the newspapers you don't read "the danger of man holding an atomic bomb," you read "the danger of the atomic bomb." This phrasing presumes that the evil has already been created, we just have to wait for it to strike.

As proof, Fromm offers two convincing pieces of evidence: The first is that the great powers—and even some lesser ones—continue to build nuclear weapons of ever greater destructive capacity, without arriving at the only sensible solution: the destruction of all nuclear weapons and of the atomic plants that supply the material. The second is that practically nothing is done to eliminate the danger of ecological catastrophe. In short, no concrete measure is taken to ensure the survival of the human species.

Hiroshima has served to introduce an extremely dangerous game for the human species: that of "playing God." It has become the symbol par excellence of man being feared as an evil god, capable of destroying hundreds of thousands of lives in a few seconds. An "invisible evil," which at any moment can manifest itself without the backing of battalions or declarations of war, an evil that feeds on "liquid fear."

Nagasaki was even worse than Hiroshima: By that time the bomb had been manufactured, it could not be wasted; although the war was ending, and although the target could not be destroyed due to reduced visibility, the bomb was dropped anyway, simply out of an "obligation to use it." The "Nagasaki syndrome" is emotional indifference, but it is also a need to do evil.

To threaten with that insidious, abominable weapon seems like a game, but it inures human beings to the prevention of evil, fostering only fear of it.

What do you think of the nuclear threat?

⸺

I THINK NUCLEAR weapons should be destroyed immediately.

The theologian Romano Guardini reflected on two forms of "inculturation."*

---

* *Incultura,* inculturation, is the acquisition of the characteristics and norms of a culture or group. In his address at the Conclusion of the Synod of Bishops at the 2015 Synod on the Family, Pope

An initial inculturation is that which the Creator gave us, so that we might transform inculturation into culture, thereby entrusting us with a great responsibility: to care for culture and make it prosper as if it were the land. I will call this inculturation "good," because it can become culture.

The second inculturation, on the other hand, is quite different: It is man who does not respect his relationship with the land, with Creation, with human beings; man who does not care for it. Developing atomic energy is not in itself negative, but using it for evil is destructive inculturation, it destroys.

I want to give a practical example: Does the death of a homeless person out in the cold in Piazza Risorgimento make the news? I don't think so. When certain bank shares fall by one percentage point, however, the news flies around the world, and everyone starts talking about how to find a solution. There you have man as the creator of inculturation and not of culture; man becomes the creator of inculturation because he does

---

Francis referred to the 1985 Synod, which he said spoke of inculturation as "the intimate transformation of authentic cultural values through their integration in Christianity, and the taking root of Christianity in the various human cultures." The "bad" inculturation described in these pages might be seen as a perversion or corruption of Christian values and principles.

not care for the environment and those who are part of it, becoming instead a slave to his own creations. Once again: Man becomes the creator of inculturation if in the scale of values the objects created by man take the place of man himself. Think of the myth of Frankenstein: Who was Frankenstein? A creature—suddenly alive—who turned against the life of the very one who created him. Another myth that explains the concept of inculturation can be found in the story of the construction of the tower of Babel: It was a magnificent tower, but some people decided to overdo it, wanted to build a tower high enough to reach God, and that was the biggest mistake. When I think of the Tower of Babel, I also think about how much labor it cost: If a brick fell from the tower you could shriek at the calamity and whoever caused it was punished mercilessly; but if a worker fell and was severely injured or died, do you know what happened? Absolutely nothing. Drawing a parallel with what happens today, think about how little outrage is now created by frequent deaths on the job—at most a "temporary" outrage, one or two days, and people are very forbearing. But think how much talk, how much haggling, takes place just to even discuss the possible enactment of a law that would somehow reduce the emission of pollutants into the atmosphere.

We need to understand that when we risk ending up in inculturation, the boundary line is very unstable, but the future of the human being depends on it, especially if we are talking about issues like the nuclear threat.

The primary characteristic of culture is "to create harmony," like nature. Inculturation, instead, is based precisely on the inability to construct harmony.

The sociologist Robert Castel pointed out: "We, at least in the countries that are said to be advanced, live in a society that is without doubt among the most secure (súres) that have ever existed." Yet, as never before, we are terrified of fear, as if the excessive security were transformed, like a boomerang, into fear of its opposite . . .

IT IS COMMON practice to believe that every achievement of power is simply progress; the fact is that modern man has not been taught the right use of power, because to all intents and purposes the immense technological growth has not advanced in step with the development of responsibility, values, and conscience. The human being has developed a power so great that it is a genuine problem; I think that managing this power is very worrying, especially if it is in the hands of a few, and in particular of people who can make unilateral decisions about how to use it.

I find the situation of young people really very worrying, because our society—especially in politics—not only confines itself to observing through a peephole, but also exploits the pain and frustration of younger generations for electoral purposes. Young people today are increasingly being led to the political extremes because politics and many media make them feel culturally and territorially threatened. Young people criticize or detest the country in which they grew up because it does not offer them a future, and they are invited daily to claim their own nationalism, shifting the target from bad politics to migrants, and more generally even toward foreigners. The young have been persuaded to embrace extremist positions, and politics has successfully shifted the problem from the "politician" to the "foreigner." Our time seems ripe for aggressive arguments, which become populist, to take root against immigrants. If we analyze the phenomenon carefully, I think young people from populist working-class or peripheral areas should be observed in particular, since they are the ones who can decide political elections; because what many media figures forget is that it is not young aristocrats who decide the fate of a country, but primarily the "uprooted" ones.

It is as if politics were using migrants as "weapons of mass distraction."

In your opinion, why do more and more young people now tend to see the greatest evil in foreigners?

I THINK THAT this phenomenon is part of a tendency toward rigidity that many young people have. Let me give you a practical example: I'm thinking of a number of young priests or students in the seminary. I've seen several of them who react to innovation and a valid diversity of views with mental rigidity rather than with wisdom. In my opinion this happens because they are frightened and because they want to force themselves to make a clear choice that will help them construct their own identity—I mean a true, unique identity, even within the Church. Nonetheless I believe that it is diversity of opinion and its expansion that profoundly enrich us and enable our society to progress, since there is nothing more useful than dialogue amid diversity. Dialogue is fruitfulness: It allows us to really know another human being in depth. Dialogue itself between young and old is a dialogue in continuity, a historical continuity, and we can also say that it is a dialogue with certain discontinuities, that is, with many-hued differences. Diversity allows us to delve into the soul and the heart: There is no white or black; there is white, black, gray, and then all the many shades of gray. We are all children of the same God; we must recognize that and be ready to accept every young person. Life itself is gray; it is a journey in search of something toward which we cannot be rigid but, as a society, proudly multicolored. A person who turns to extremes and tends toward rigidity is a fearful person: He hides behind rigidity as a defense.

Behind and under every rigidity there is always an unresolved problem and also, perhaps, an illness. A humble attitude, open to others, the attitude of those who can listen, protects us from rigidity. Humility is a favor that we do for ourselves. Rigidity is the easiest reaction to the torrent of life that propels us forward.

The same thing happens with immigrants. We don't ask ourselves why this human being has come here, whether he is fleeing from a war, whether we would have done the same thing in his place. A rigid individual simply has one refrain in his head: *He's a foreigner and should go back to where he came from!*

Do you know what I think of when I see an immigrant? First of all, I think of my immigrant father. And then I ask myself this question: Why them and not me? And I repeat it again: Why them and not me? Any one of us could be in their situation: We should always put ourselves in someone else's place, learn to walk in their shoes, think about how it would be if we didn't even have the money to buy those shoes.

If God has granted us the chance to live a better life, why don't we thank Him and try to put ourselves in the place of those who are less fortunate than us? We must feel responsible for our neighbor. How wonderful it would be if each of us began asking ourselves: "What can I do to alleviate the suffering of others, whether they are fellow countrymen or foreigners?" Instead, unfortunately, people who are rigid have only one question in their heads: "What can I do to get rid of him?" The same thing happens with new ideas: The rigid individual is unable to even accept the fact that they exist.

If, on the one hand, populist opposition toward immigrants is worrying, on the other hand, it is nice to see the generosity of some nations toward the cause: for example, Italy and Greece, among others. They are also the closest countries geographically, it's true, but what matters is that they have accepted these immigrants, they were willing to welcome them, inclined to be altruistic; that is really the bottom line and what should make the citizens of these countries proud: They have shown the world the merit of being hospitable.

Then, too, there is another problem, which is a real tragedy. I spoke about it recently with two heads of state: Europe has no children. We are in full demographic winter yet, despite this situation, some don't want people from other countries to come here. Do we want a deserted Europe? Only France registers a high number of newborns, thanks mainly to assistance to families to encourage births, but obviously that is not enough to avoid having a barren Europe.

Sometimes couples think more urgently about planning vacations than creating a family; are they perhaps afraid to leave the future in the hands of their heirs, heirs who would in fact be a testimony to the greatness of their love?

I cannot conceive of such a fear . . .

We have a responsibility to generate life; as citizens we must populate our country. I feel like saying, jokingly, if we don't want to do it ourselves, then leave it to others!

In any case it is true, many young people take up rigid positions in the trenches of fear, and this is a tendency we must deal with.

Some time ago I was at a conference dedicated to the risks related to the lack of privacy online. In particular, a speaker was explaining to the younger ones, an entire middle school, that once photos posted on social media appear online—whether it be Facebook, Instagram, Snapchat, or any other platform—they are no longer owned by the photographer and the subject of the photograph, but become in all respects the property of the managers of the social network, who can view them as often as they want. A loud murmur was immediately heard in the front row, and the speaker asked the least hesitant-looking boy the reason for it. His response was truly unexpected and, in some ways, revolutionary: "Can Facebook really notice us? Can my photos actually be seen by those who run the site, who may even decide to show them to others? That's terrific: I'm going to post more of my photos." All of his classmates seemed enthusiastic about his statement. What immediately appeared clear to me once again was the enormous gap between adults, worried about being spied on, and the very young generations, worried that they are not seen enough. If this were to be confirmed over time, the uprooted society would have an absolutely new aspect: the pointlessness of privacy and the need for its opposite.

One of today's greatest fears is invisibility, not being able to be seen . . .

=====

I THINK WHAT you tell me is normal in our narcissistic culture; it does not surprise me. The narcissistic culture has been gradually increasing in society, to the degree of directly involving children in the primary grades and secondary schools. And I see how this can even change people's brains; the brain changes, it alters. *Appearance* becomes more important, therefore, than *being*, indeed from the earliest age.

When you were young, what did it mean to be afraid? What were you afraid of?

=====

I HAD A great fear when I was young: a fear of not being loved.

I see a certain similarity, albeit indirect, between the fear of invisibility and the fear of not being loved: If I am not visible I cannot be appreciated and consequently I cannot feel loved . . . Can it be that today we need large numbers to feel loved—we've gone global with our private problems—whereas previously we were satisfied with the love of fewer people?

Perhaps the process is similar, but the fear of being invisible is something that young people are hardly aware of; it is more an unconscious fear. I was very aware of my fear of not being loved.

How did you overcome the fear of not being loved?

I BELIEVE I overcame it by seeking authenticity: I saw that I would never do anything that wasn't authentic, not even to buy the love and esteem of others. I also fought against "the society of appearance," and I continue to do so by accepting myself for what I am and by reflecting on an image that I often think of. "The society of appearance" is built on vanity, and what is the symbol par excellence of vanity? The peacock. Think about the peacock: When people picture this creature, they see it with its open tail fan of colorful feathers. But the reality is not that. Do you want to see the reality of the peacock? Walk around it and look at it from behind. Vanity is always two-faced. Authenticity is the way to salvation because it brings you people's esteem; if people value you for what you really are, then you will feel loved, you'll see. Being loved is one of the consequences of authenticity.

In our liquid society, and for young people who are also uprooted, anxiety and depression have increased, but the Epicurean ideal ("live in obscurity") has nearly disappeared. Yet the cure for these two evils could be invisibility. Precisely that invisibility that today appears to be the worst modern social "disease." If you are not visible online, you have little chance of climbing the social pyramid, no chance to shop around for romance. What would you say to a young person who is a victim of anxiety and depression and who, feeling invisible, is unable to find dignity and meaning in his life?

WE ALL HAVE dignity in the eyes of God and only He can see it deep within, looking beyond all our mistakes and all our flaws. God not only asks us what we did and where we were, He also asks us where we are now and who we will be. He wants to heal our wounds, and here I want to bring up another aspect that relates to depression and anxiety: God wants young people to have a purpose. The cure for anxiety and depression comes from having a mission. Earlier I said that young people are prophets, perhaps the most important prophets of the world. The mission of young people is to be prophets and to be prophets they have to "get their feet dirty" in the streets, they have to be among other young people in search of meaning and help them, they have to become bearers of hope and become independent from adults. If young people struggle daily to improve this world, starting with small things, they will be able to get out of the state of almost absolute dependency on adults. They must stand together, join forces, respect one another, and have a clear objective: a mission, to be exact. Being missionaries, in the broad sense of the word, allows us to observe the world with new eyes, no longer as tourists in life, but as protagonists. The Devil strives for competition, division; he would like the young to be divided and lost in this society, depressed and anxious; the Devil wants every young person to be alone against everyone. The Lord, on the other hand, wants young people to unite; He seeks them out and He does so to offer each of them His hand. The Lord scolds us for the weaknesses that stem from our lack of hope, so hope must be the foundation of every day; we must never fall into the abyss of depression, and we must remember that at times a tiny glimmer is enough to begin to hope again. To be more precise, the darker it is, the more perceptible a tiny glimmer can be.

When we talk about anxiety and depression, however, we should not confuse these feelings with impatience and disquiet, because every human being has two types of restlessness, one good and one bad. The good one is the restlessness that the Holy Spirit bestows on us, which causes the soul to be anxious to do good things, to be constructive, while the bad one arises from a sick, dirty conscience and eats away at the person who carries it in his blood. I once talked of a constant itching on the part of those who live with bad anxiety . . . It's an image that I'm thinking about even now.

How does one become malicious? What are the roots of evil?

I ALWAYS SPEAK of the three roots par excellence of evil: greed, vanity, and pride.

From an early age one experiences malice. What strikes you about the phenomenon of "bullying," and its online offshoots, cyberbullying and trolling?

═══

I AM STRUCK by the human being's need to be aggressive. It's as if it were an actual necessity; it happens among children and among adults.

In the Bible there is the story of the twins Esau and Jacob: Even in the womb their mother felt the twins struggle to overpower each other. During their lives they fought constantly; they became enemies, then friends, then enemies again. When we talk about bullying I immediately think of those two brothers in the Bible, because they represent so well what I mean by the need to be aggressive. The first to be born was Esau and soon after, Jacob. Isaac's legacy and blessing would therefore by right go to Esau, according to the law of primogeniture. The years go by. Esau is now a tall young man, sturdy as an oak; Jacob, on the other hand, is thin and submissive. Esau is a skilled hunter, Jacob not so much. One day Jacob cooks a lentil stew. Esau comes home from the countryside, tired and hungry. He says to his brother: "Let me gulp down some of that red stuff; I am famished." Jacob takes advantage of the situation. The birthright was important to him. He ardently wanted to receive Isaac's blessing. So he says to his brother, "First sell me your right as firstborn." Esau replies, "Look, I am on the point of dying. What good is the right as firstborn to me?" So Esau sells his birthright to his twin brother under oath for a plate of lentil stew (Genesis 25:29–34). This passage can be an opening to the topic of bullying: You see, bullying is invented by violence. And what Jacob did is also an example of violence.

Speaking about wars with a head of state, I said that we live in an era characterized by a cruelty perhaps never before seen, but his answer was: "Holy Father, this cruelty has always existed; it simply wasn't so visible."

Bullying has entered a very important phase in its history; I can affirm that today it is even more widespread than before, even if it has always existed. And it is more widespread, not because we see it on the Web and there are conferences that talk about it, but because it is part of the superficiality of the throwaway culture that invades us. Even among children there is already a tendency to consume, to discard, and throw away what they have *consumed,* and to have no qualms about doing so.

Have you ever been bullied?

————

PERSONALLY, NO, BUT I have seen what it means to experience it in some classmates who were very close to me. Even today I talk with a middle-school classmate of mine who was constantly targeted by other students and often picked on. He overcame those problems, but he suffered greatly because of it. We must always regard others with empathy and hope. Empathy and hope. And all it takes is just one good individual for there to be hope.

Young people today should have many more opportunities than their peers a few decades ago had—just think about the Web, which has firmly established the supremacy of time over space, or about fast modes of travel—yet they come out of these experiences much more frustrated. They are illustrations that support the dictum "If you can do it, you must do it" and the consequent loss. It's like constantly watching a feast of delicacies but being tied to a chair at least three yards away. You think: "I can see what I'm missing—it's ending up in someone else's mouth—but it's my destiny to get used to this torment." To make matters worse, it's possible to know practically everything about those who are banqueting in your place—thanks to the Internet and social media—and this makes the cognitive dissonance even more unbearable.

They are in effect frustrated generations, and frustrated individuals, according to most research studies in social psychology, produce aggression. Aggression that today becomes entertainment more than anything. Evil no longer needs to be justified; it becomes routine.

What are your thoughts on all this?

I THINK THAT you have described the situation well. And it is all related once again to bullying and the need to be aggressive that I spoke of earlier. Let's take the story of Cain and Abel: Jealousy drove Cain to commit an extreme injustice against his brother. This in turn caused a rupture in the relationship between Cain and God and between Cain and the land, from which he was exiled. This passage is summarized in the conversation between God and Cain. God asks: "Where is your brother Abel?" Cain says he does not know, and God insists: "What have you done? Your brother's blood cries out to me from the ground! Now you are banned from [this] ground" (Genesis 4:9–11). And here I want to return to a very important concept: Neglecting the obligation to cultivate and maintain a proper relationship with my neighbor, whom I have a duty to care for and look after, destroys my inner relationship with myself, with others, with God, and with the earth. When these relationships are neglected, when justice no longer dwells on earth, the Bible tells us that all life is in danger. This is what the story of Noah teaches us, when God threatens to wipe out humanity because of its persistent inability to live up to the demands of justice and peace: "I see that the end of all mortals has come, for the earth is full of lawlessness because of them" (Genesis 6:13). In these stories there was already a strong conviction, everlastingly current: Everything is related, everything is integrated and in motion, the care of our life and our relationship with nature is inseparable from fraternity, justice, and devotion toward others.

You recalled the story of Cain and Abel. Would you like to send a message to young people in prison, perhaps sentenced to life imprisonment?

———

PUNISHMENT SHOULD NEVER deprive the punished of hope: This is why I am against both the death penalty and life imprisonment interpreted as "forever." There are countries where the death penalty is legal and torture is common. I would like to tell all the heads of state, every person all over the world to reflect on this every day: To deprive a human being of even the slightest possibility of hope is killing him two, three, four, five times. It means killing him multiple times a day, every day of his life. It is truly very sad to teach people, from the time they are children, that hope does not exist. If you end up on death row there is no hope; if they condemn you to life imprisonment there is no hope, and this is profoundly wrong: There must always

be hope in our lives, and therefore in every punishment.

How does one find hope?

———

I WOULD SAY to young Christians: by seeking Jesus,
knowing that He listens to us, knowing that everything
has meaning in His eyes. Let us ask Him for hope, and
let us do it with the rosary in our hands, as humble servants of good. Sometimes I hear young Catholics who
think they are too busy to pray and talk with Our Lady
and Jesus; I tell them to find fifteen minutes to talk
with the heart. If you talk to the Madonna with your
heart, you are always heard. It is an act of love that you
can do for yourself: The way you focus on your smart-
phone, you can focus on the rosary even for a few minutes. Or you can even download an application with a
virtual rosary and pray that way: Our Lady does not
pay attention to the form, but to the substance; it's not
a problem. Our Lady pays attention to sincere hearts.

But I would like to return to the message for a young
person serving a life term: It is essential that a prisoner
have the opportunity to re-enter society, even if only
for a short time, to perform useful work, to understand
that he has done wrong and to try to feel of use to the

community. Feeling absolutely useless is a terrible evil, which can lead to worse acts. Feeling useful, on the other hand, offers hope. I often go to prisons, even maximum security facilities, where there are prisoners with dozens of murders behind them. In several of them I was struck by the administration's ability to convey hope. I saw women wardens who were very good; they acted as if they were the prisoners' mothers; they gave them hope and praised the inmates for each step forward they took toward understanding their errors and being of use to others. I saw women superintendents who are perhaps able to manage conflicts better than men, and I believe it derives from a woman's proclivity to motherhood.

What do you say to young inmates when you go to the prisons?

TO BEGIN WITH, I am saddened when I see that some inmates will most likely never leave the prison. My first emotion is definitely sorrow. If I find a young man in prison, I know that my mission is to give him hope; my usefulness is the same as that of any other visitor who wishes this prisoner to understand his mistakes in order to transform the evil he has done into good toward others. There is no human being who lacks the ability to do good toward others; we are all potential creators of good. Every human being who is *lost* is one less human being to bring about "the revolution of good." Every person *wasted* is a defeat for all humanity. Generally when I visit the inmates I don't talk much; instead I let them talk, I let this happen naturally, leaving them free to express themselves.

Must hope necessarily come from faith in God?

NOT NECESSARILY. THERE can be, I would say, an "agnostic hope," a "human hope." As I said, one good individual is enough to give hope. In any case, God sees all the good that a person does and thinks. If you create hope, even the punishment of prison does not create a wall. Walls bring with them an incurable evil: the absence of dialogue and the destruction of society. Walls must be torn down with dialogue and with love. If you are talking and someone puts up a wall, then speak louder so the one on the other side of the wall will still hear you and will be able to answer you. If you do good, don't be afraid to shout. Doing good must become an addiction, an addiction that you must not recover from.

There are also harmful addictions, though: I'm thinking about young people addicted to drugs and alcohol. What is your message for them? And what are drugs today?

———

I THINK THAT today these addictions are a form of discarding. I think they can be a social cruelty used by the powerful, sometimes consciously, and that a person doesn't become an addict only because of his fragility. I think much more could be done on an international level to limit the spread of drugs, but corruption is too widespread to be able to stop it without a change in global culture. The best way—I would even say the only way—to act quickly is prevention in the very young, before it becomes an addiction.

Your question also makes me think of a phrase from Fromm: "Modern capitalism needs men who cooperate smoothly and in large numbers; who want to consume more and more; and whose tastes are standardized and can be easily influenced and anticipated. It needs men who feel free and independent, not subject to any authority or principle or conscience—yet willing to be commanded, to do what is expected of them, to fit into the social machine without friction; who can be guided without force, led without leaders, prompted without aim—except the one to make good, to be on the move, to function, to go ahead."

Today the world wants the young to conform—it wants young people who are all the same, young people who imitate other young people to construct an identity. Those who aren't in step with this system are sometimes tempted to resort to something artificial. We talked earlier about plastic surgery, which is somewhat related to this. Drugs fit into this context as well, though they are not a perfect comparison: They are a weak individual's response to his inability and failure to conform. He can't successfully conform; he would like to, but he knows that he is not capable of it or that he would not be accepted in any case. So he moves on to the "plastic surgery of the brain" phase: He constructs a way of thinking that he knows is not his, but that is the only one he thinks can enable him to survive. He relies on the "eternal temporary," which he knows is the end for him, but he does it anyway; he settles for the moments when he is out of it, though he knows that it will cost him dearly. When I say the word *conformity,* I think about how grave the danger of homologizing thought is. I think it is much more dangerous to homologize thinking than to try to revolutionize it. Here I like to make a very clear distinction between what I call "single thought," which is "weak" thought, as compared to "strong" thinking.

"Single thought" is the offspring of an actual sociocultural situation: It is what unfortunately seems to dominate the world and also legitimizes the presence of "death sentences" and true "human sacrifices." Single thought arises from "spherical globalization," which holds that everyone should be the same, that they should conform. Those who promote this, however, forget that we cannot talk about globalization without respecting each individual's identity; true globalization is polyhedral, not spherical.

Theories that the uprooted society, with its throwaway culture, consistently wants to impose are part of single thought. There is a prophetic novel, written in 1907 by Robert Hugh Benson, entitled *Lord of the World,* which closely describes the method of an invasive culture that abolishes the possibility of thinking autonomously. I believe that our era is effectively one of single thought, and it is vital and urgent to disrupt this thought via creative imagination. The dreams of the elderly are a very strong example of desires that disrupt single thought; if joined with the courage of the young, with their prophecy, they can truly shatter the homologation of thought.

Single thought is weak because it is not genuine, it is not personal; it is imposed, and as a result probably no one feels it as his own. Everyone tends to live it, but without thinking about it. Strong thought, instead, is the creative kind, and we must always aspire to this. To homologize thought is to live within a "bubble," leading to autism of the intellect, of feeling. A great many ills can arise from these grave maladies of the human being . . .

In your opinion, is it more common for the drug addict to be discarded by society, or is it being discarded that leads to developing addictions such as drugs?

———

I THINK THAT feeling discarded by society leads to developing addictions. Although that is not always the case: Sometimes too much money leads to the search for new experiences and addictions, including drugs. Those who take drugs are always running away, creating a world they can escape to. They seek and accept a fake world, one of illusions, a world that is foreign to concrete reality.

Why do human beings fear death so much?

———

DEATH IS VIEWED by human beings as a threat, a challenge to confront.

As a young man, the doctors diagnosed me with

lung cysts, and for the first time I felt a fear of dying. It was anguish, something mysterious, a brush with the end, yet I was so young. The two images are so rationally distant, youth and death, yet I went through both; the experience intensely disoriented me. Stricken, I looked at my mother, hugged her, and said, "Mama, what's going to happen to me? Am I going to die?" It was an extremely difficult period.

Fear of death is fear of total annihilation: Only those who have faith in the hereafter are able to trust. When I speak about death with atheists, or self-proclaimed ones, delving a little deeper into their atheism, I find that in many of them there is a recurring reference to the afterlife, to what some call an energy, which unites us all.

I remember a man who because of some of his assertions was very important to me. He collected payments on the electric and gas bills; he did it door-to-door, one of those jobs that no longer exist. One day, talking about death, he told me: "I'm not afraid of death once it's here; my fear is to see it coming . . ."

This is another reason why I want to stress that it is very difficult to be happy without a sense of humor; we must be capable of not taking ourselves too seriously.

Instances of suicide, especially in these times of crisis, are the order of the day. If you had the opportunity to talk to someone who was about to perform that extreme act, what would you say to him?

———

I WOULD LOOK into his eyes, I would talk about the heart, mine and his . . . On this subject I want to say that a person who commits suicide is a victim. Of himself, of his sins perhaps, or of a mental illness, of social conditioning, or other contingent, influential factors. A hypocrite, on the other hand, is more of a suicide: He commits suicide every day; he kills his morality and his dignity, and lives by appearances. The hypocrites are the real suicides to condemn . . .

I'm thinking about exploited young people who come from different countries, but also about young prostitutes who arrive from Africa, from Eastern Europe, from South America, and from other European countries as well. They are used as sex slaves, and in the most ruthless way. Often we read that they are tricked into being transported from the country where they were born, deceived about a better future, kidnapped, confined, drugged, thrown onto the roadside to struggle to survive. Is there anything that young people can do for these young women?

=====

Yes, approach them not to exploit them, but to talk to them. Go up to them and instead of asking "How much do you want?" ask "How much are you suffering?" It is part of young people's mission to go out into the streets and, as I said before, "get their feet dirty." Often we do not realize how important small acts are; acts that may seem like negligible, trifling gestures will actually be gigantic in the eyes of God and of those in need. Young people must not tire of finding ways to talk with those who live on the streets, and with those who need them; every young person must do it in his own way, without following a written bureaucratic procedure. There are no universal procedures for doing good, but there are many personal, effective interpretations as testaments to their goodness.

You speak quite often of mercy . . .

=====

It is one of the aspects of God that I love to talk about most, because it is probably the Lord's strongest message. The Lord is a Father "rich in mercy" (Ephesians 2:4). What I mean is that young people have a Father who is always watching over them with a benevolent and merciful gaze, a Father who is not in competition with them, a Father who at all times awaits them with open arms. And this is a certainty that, if you embrace it, instills hope and consolation in every human being, and is very effective in battling depression.

The parable of the lost son (Luke 15:11–24) is very well known, but it is always helpful to read it again:

Then [the Lord Jesus] said, "A man had two sons, and the younger son said to his father, 'Father, give me the share of your estate that should come to me.' So the father divided the property between them. After a few days, the younger son collected all his belongings and set off to a distant country where he squandered his inheritance on a life of dissipation. When he had freely spent everything, a severe famine struck that country, and he found himself in dire need. So he hired himself out to one of the local citizens who sent him to his farm to tend the swine. And he longed to eat his fill of the pods on which the swine fed, but nobody gave him any. Coming to his senses he thought, 'How many of my father's hired workers have more than enough food to eat, but here am I, dying from hunger. I shall get up and go to my father and I shall say to him, "Father, I have sinned against Heaven and against you. I no longer deserve to be called your son; treat me as you would treat one of your hired workers."' So he got up and went back to his father. While he was still a long way off, his father caught sight of him, and was filled with compassion. He ran to his son, embraced him and kissed him. His son said to him, 'Father, I have sinned against Heaven and against you; I no longer deserve to be called your son.' But his father ordered his servants, 'Quickly bring the finest robe and put it on him; put a ring on his finger and sandals on his feet. Take the fattened calf and slaughter it. Then let us celebrate with a feast, because this son of mine was dead, and has come to life again; he was lost, and has been found.' Then the celebration began."

The only thing that can temporarily separate us from God is our sin. So, once again, we are the only ones who can decide to distance ourselves from God; He never decides to distance Himself from us. If, however, we acknowledge our sin, confess it sincerely, and repent, that sin becomes a meeting ground: because He is mercy and awaits us in that very place.

PART III

TEACHING IS LEARNING

When you look at children, do you ever fear for their future?

=====

IN CHILDREN, I see the future, prosperity. Sometimes just looking at them moves me. I try not to be influenced by thoughts that go beyond the image I have before me: The joy that a child's smile transmits to us can be a cure even for adults. When I see a child, I see tenderness, and where there is tenderness, destruction cannot enter.

I like to recount a recent experience of mine, during the Wednesday audiences: I had a delightful, happy, smiling child in front of me. A young man was holding him in his arms, trying to keep an eye on him as he made him drink from a bottle of milk. Beside them was the child's mother, paralyzed, in a wheelchair. I approached and immediately sensed the joy all three of them felt in this scene: The father looked at me, beaming, and I thanked him for having graced me with such a happy sight. I complimented him, but the young man instantly told me that the entire credit was due to his wife, not to him: "She does it all." I hurriedly greeted the woman as well, who looked at me with a brilliant smile, exclaiming: "Bless me because I am about to have another . . . ," and she pointed to her belly, which was beginning to show. There it was, a scene of fruitfulness, love that overcomes every obstacle, that makes us see how great God is, how sturdy and marvelous is the hope He gives us. We must be able to perceive this hope, to accept it and transform it into the joy of living. This is an exercise that we can do each day.

When we talk about the attributes that a parent must never lack, I say: tenderness, a predisposition to listen, to always take their children seriously, and above all to be willing and able to "guide" them. This is a very important verb: Children have their own lives; parents can guide them in their choices, but not make them for them. Guiding children in their choices is a great opportunity for parents, not a limitation.

A child's smile, the open smile of a child who puts his trust in his parents . . . is something that does me a lot of good, that can do everyone good. And I find many similarities between that smile and that of the elderly. Both are open to life, from opposite extremes, from the beginning and from the end: It is an outlook that unites them.

Let's talk about ways to transmit knowledge: Which are the most effective ones, and which can be dangerous?

————

THIS QUESTION REMINDS me of the great difference that exists between genuine myth—which is a contemplative mode that helps open our eyes to the mystery of reality—and the creation of stories to justify a reality that seeks to impose itself. Myth is a way to know the truth—in the Bible, for example, numerous "myths" are used to lead us to the truth—and it is universal; on the other hand, a narration, a story—and here I'm talking about it as a form of knowledge—is constructed to pass off as true what probably isn't. A story is a justification, always. Imagine a corporate leader who managed to attain power, perhaps in an illicit way. What does he do? He constructs an "epic tale," he resorts to an *ad personam* narration to cleanse his conscience. He covers up his life with a story. If you think about it, speaking through stories is a characteristic of this liquid society.

This reflection of yours makes me think about how fairy tales for children have changed so much: Today more real-life stories are popular, rather than the famous Aesop's fables—symbolic par excellence—that my generation grew up with. Is there a myth that every young person should read right now?

=====

THE MYTH OF Narcissus, certainly, but also that of Icarus. These myths are the first that come to mind: It is right to be daring, especially if you are young, but you must be at least as prudent. Icarus thought in terms of the moment, he did not consider time: This is also the message of that myth. As you can see, every myth requires interpretation; it delves into human experience and tries to find analogies. It stimulates the imagination and also leads to dialogue: A myth can be interpreted for years and years, because when it comes to myths we don't debate, we discuss. Myths do not depend solely on the story or solely on the imagination; they contain something closely linked to men's lives, to experience, to what our forefathers have handed down to us, something that never grows old, like time. Myths do not grow old because they are essentially linked to human nature: They can be interpreted even after decades, centuries, and millennia; that is another reason why I think myths must again play a central role in the transmission of knowledge.

What are the characteristics of a good educator? I mean both a good schoolteacher and a good parent . . .

═══

A GOOD EDUCATOR asks himself this question every day: "Is my heart open enough today to allow surprise to enter?" Educating isn't just explaining theories; it is above all an exchange of views, making dialogic thinking triumph. A good educator wants to learn something every day from his students, from his children. There is no such thing as one-way education; there is only two-way education. I teach you, but while I am doing so you are teaching me something, maybe something even more useful than what I am teaching you. If I, the educator, am teaching you theories, you, who are listening to me, are teaching me how you adopt them in practice and how you interpret them individually, how you bring them into the world, combining them with your personality and your previous experiences. We all have something to teach, but also much to learn: We must never forget that, at every age, every season of life.

Yet today's culture fosters transience . . .

═══

LET US ASK ourselves what transience really is: It is the predominance of the *moment* over *time*. Time moves forward, but the moment is locked in itself, it stands still. I like to draw a distinction between transience, which revolves around the concept of the moment, and the absolute, which is what I mean by time and which never stands still. The moment is more like space than time. Let's think about space: It is solid; it has a well-defined, visible beginning; and we know that it ends. How often, when looking at a specific space, do we have to look for where it ends? The moment is similar, it "burns" itself up in its own voracity; it is finite and defined. It is different, instead, to think of time as life, as evolution, as opening up to the experiences of existence. The moment never presupposes evolution, time does. Transience has a fleeting nature because it is closed in itself, it is a slave to moments; nowadays, there is a tendency to cling to the provisional, to moments, to accept them as "illusory eternity." Time always moves ahead, toward the absolute.

We must also watch out for another error of interpretation: the danger of living in the moment as if it were time. I remember a brilliant young man who many years ago suddenly decided he wanted to become a priest . . . but only for ten years! He did not feel up to committing to any more: This is the culture of the moment. Even when a person uses phrases like "I want this for a lifetime," in many cases he is talking only of the moment, thinking that he is in time; immaturity can often lead one to confuse these two aspects.

What words should a good educator or a good parent never say?

═════

IN REFERENCE TO education, this is probably the worst, whether it is an elementary, middle-school, high school, or university teacher or any parent who says it: "What do you know about it, kid? Read up and then we'll talk about it."

What does forgiveness mean to you?

═════

I AM REMINDED of when, as a little boy, I had a big argument with an aunt I was very fond of. I said very mean things to her during that quarrel, things that I didn't really mean; I wanted to hurt her. In the following days I felt that if I did not humbly ask her for forgiveness, I would lose something on a personal level: I would destroy my dignity, I would be inauthentic. I chose to be authentic and, having asked my aunt for forgiveness, from that day on I was loved by her even more than before. We must learn to see forgiveness as an act of healthy selfishness, not just altruism. It is also an act of healthy selfishness because you want to be authentic for yourself, often more so than for others. We must teach children to act honorably.

You often bring up the parable of the Good Samaritan: Does every good deed of ours, like that of the Good Samaritan, arise out of love for our neighbor, or more out of a desire to be well thought of?

———

MOST LIKELY, AT least at the outset, no one does things just out of good intentions—technically we say "with rectitude of intention"—but I would say that it is not that important to know whether, at the start of an action, good arises from healthy selfishness or pure altruism; what matters is to do good and produce good. Doing good leads to good. And rectitude of intention grows; it is continually purified.

I would like to talk about children's tendency to "cast aside" their parents, perceiving themselves as independent very early on, and about their precocious, growing need for a private sphere apart from the family, while at the same time they are paradoxically opening up to the world, with the obliteration of privacy that this requires.
  Parents will know their children more through their online pres-

ence than their offline presence, just as they do their children's friends, their classmates. For the first time in the history of humanity, children will be the teachers of many parents. This is a phenomenon that we are already witnessing to some extent. Does Google know more or does my dad know more? The child just has to ask the same question of Google and of his parents, and with a few clicks he will see how much more certain and more rewarding it is to listen to Google, which will increasingly become an inseparable and above all, reliable and silent friend, since none of the child's friends will ever know how much Google's advice shaped his learning.

In contrast, asking a parent presumes an implicit judgment of the child's preparation on that particular topic. And it can have consequences, psychological at least, on the child and on the parent-child relationship.

The real problem with all this is that if we add it all up, we see the creation of a dizzying gap between those with power today and those who will instead have it tomorrow. So if the crisis we are experiencing today continues—and there is no sign of any change in course—the generations to come will have much greater capability and much less opportunity. More capability and fewer jobs. The danger is that when there are five or six discarded generations and they, inevitably, hold power, they will attach less importance to democracy, since it betrayed their ideals, and embrace new forms of government, such as authoritarianism.

Is there still time to stop a course like this?

THIS HISTORICAL PERIOD is a crucial time to avoid what you are talking about, which would certainly be the worst evil. And it is today that we urgently need to raise the banner of dialogue, of constructive dialogue, between the young and old. Our young people want to feel like protagonists, and they try to act like protagonists. But since adults do not allow them to occupy their natural place, it is the support of the elderly that can allow young people freedom. The young definitely do not like to feel commanded or like they have to respond to "orders" that come from the adult world, so it is also up to the elderly to speak to the young in the right way. Young people seek that supportive autonomy that makes them feel like they are "their own boss." In this we can find good opportunities, especially through schools, parishes, and ecclesiastical movements. It is the duty of us all to encourage activities that put young people to the test, that make them feel like protagonists. The dangers you expressed are very frightening, and for that reason we must act right now, with a genuine cultural revolution of dialogue.

We live in a relentless context of consumerism; it compels us to an "all-consuming consumption." Therefore it is urgent that we reclaim an important and undervalued spiritual principle: austerity. We have entered an abyss of consumption where we are led to believe that we are valued for what we are capable of producing and consuming, for what we are able to possess. Educating about austerity actually results in an incomparable richness. It awakens the intellect and creativity, generates opportunities for imagination, and, in particular, leads to teamwork and solidarity. Contrast this with a kind of "spiritual gluttony" where, rather than eating, gluttons devour everything around them, they gorge themselves. I think we should educate ourselves better, as families, as communities, to make room for austerity as a way to come together, to build bridges, to open up spaces, to grow with others and for others.

In the apostolic exhortation *Amoris Laetitia* I said: "The life of every family is marked by all kinds of crises, yet these are also part of its dramatic beauty. Couples should be helped to realize that surmounting a crisis need not weaken their relationship; instead, it can improve, settle and mature the wine of their union. Life together should not diminish but increase their contentment; every new step along the way can help couples find new ways to happiness" (no. 232). I feel it is important to undertake the education of children from this perspective, as a calling from the Lord to us, as a family; to make each step one of growth; and to learn to better savor the gift of life that He gives us.

When can one feel truly free?

=====

ONE IS FREE only if one is in harmony with oneself.

Freedom, and therefore harmony, cannot be created in a laboratory: They are part of a human path of introspection, of a journey. This path can be steep and arduous, but if the journey is made with sincerity and purity, the reward is harmony.

Young people often feel betrayed, even by university. In many cases, a degree nowadays seems to be a license to be unemployed. Knowledge seems to be increasingly disengaged from profit, from economic gain. But knowledge and intellectual curiosity continue to be fundamental, and even more so in the liquid society. How can we nurture the desire to learn in young people who feel betrayed?

=====

TRUE CULTURE HAS three languages. That of the head, which is what some universities use today— maybe to train unemployed professionals, as you say; then there is the language of the heart; and finally, the language of the hands, that of action. It is extremely crucial that education and those who work in education are able to employ and harmonize all three of these languages. "Learn what you feel and do"; "Feel what you think and do"; "Do what you think and feel."

Everything must be connected; it must be integrated, systematic, and mobile, flexible. Things can no longer be static as before. We must be more honest with students. Today you cannot work with a young person without helping him to feel and without helping him to *do*. We must, as I said, be in motion, always. "Studying" must encompass "thinking" together with "doing" and "feeling."

Many times we demand an excessive education from students in certain fields that we consider important. We ask them to learn a number of things so they can give it "their best shot." But we do not give equal weight to the fact that they know their country, that they love their roots, and above all, that they *do*.

Young students seek in many ways the "giddiness" that makes them feel alive. So let's give it to them! Let's inspire them; let's help them transform their dreams into projects. Let us spare no effort so that they can discover that all the potential they have is a bridge, a transition to a vocation, in the broadest and most beautiful sense of the word. Let's offer them overarching goals, significant challenges, and help them to accomplish them, to reach them. Let's not leave them on their own; let's challenge them more than they challenge us.

Let's help young people grow up soundly anti-conformist! Let's not let them get the "giddiness" from those who only put their lives at risk: Let's give it to them ourselves! This obviously requires finding educators capable of committing themselves to children's growth. To educate today's adolescents we cannot continue to use a teaching model that is merely scholastic, consisting only of ideas. We must follow the pace of young people's growth. It is important to help them cultivate self-esteem, to believe that they can really succeed in what they set themselves to do.

If we want our children to be educated and prepared for tomorrow, they will not succeed by learning scholastic material alone. It is necessary for them to *connect,* to know their roots. Only in this way will they be able to soar high, otherwise they will be caught up in other people's "visions."

When we talk about the transmission of knowledge in our postmodern age, it is almost inevitable that we talk about post-truth and fake news. What are your thoughts about this?

IN ONE OF our meetings I had the opportunity to reflect on how social networks today are, in effect, true dictionaries of sociology. It is incredible how easy it is in the era of post-truth to mistake fake news for real news, but above all, and this is probably the most interesting aspect, even when that news is declared "fake" to all effects and purposes, the conversation about that "fact" continues just the same; as if merely by having been created, albeit falsely, that communication has every right to still provoke a reaction in people. Many people don't care whether the news is true or fake; what counts is that someone created it, what matters is the emotion that it aroused in the specific user; that is more than enough to keep it "alive," on the surge of a constant flow of diverse opinions.

Analyzing numerous cases of post-truth and fake news related to immigrants, for example, I confirmed one thing: The gap between the middle class, which is increasingly between the lower-middle and the upper class—by which I mean the categories of politicians, managers, wealthy entrepreneurs, and so-called VIPs—has widened considerably; as a result, if you are part of the lower-middle group, one way to keep your identity as intact as possible seems to be to make sure, not so much that you try to rise to the level of those "above" you, but that there is someone still "below" you.

And this is a very significant change in perspective, in our era.

Fear of seeing rights guaranteed to those who are poorer sparks the same frustration that, as a general rule, should have been directed toward those who caused the gap to widen.

This frustration lacks the drive to fight for a cause that seems lost from the start, for a gap that is becoming unbridgeable; consequently, as a defense mechanism—Freud could come to the rescue with several of his theories—this frustration unleashes its force in hatred toward the immigrant.

If I say the word "group," what does it bring to mind?

TODAY THE WORD "swarm" could, in some cases, be a substitute for the word "group."

It is rare for individuals to spontaneously form cohesive, hierarchical groups with genuine leaders; this happens less and less often. Instead what we see more and more is people gathering intermittently, coming together and scattering in a short time, not sharing but accompanying one another, driven by motives that are ephemeral and by objectives that are constantly changing. And here I refer to sociologist Zygmunt Bauman, who writes: "The seductive power of mobile objectives is a rule sufficient to coordinate movements, and this is enough to render superfluous any other command or imposition from above."

This is highly compatible with the style of the Web, which tends to be "gaseous."

And doesn't fashion also produce constant "swarms," like those of insects?

Even the above-mentioned plastic surgery produces "swarms."

These are all "non-spaces" from which anyone can leave, return, scatter, where each person pursues his own individual interest that only marginally coincides with that of the others, where there is no hierarchy and where there is no sharing, only fleeting accompaniment.

Is being ambitious a defect or a virtue?

===

CERTAINLY A TOTAL lack of ambition is a defect.

The important thing is that ambition not become a way of trampling on others in order to get ahead and continue climbing. Climbers are the worst individuals because they tend to produce—with great ease— inculturation, a bad culture.

I instead support ambition that is consistent with respect for others, especially the weak. I would like to see ambitious, courageous, anti-conformist, and revolutionary young people who show tenderness.

In connection with this, what do you expect from the Synod on Young People?

＝＝＝

I EXPECT THEM to be the protagonists. The Synod is an assembly of bishops, but it must be at the service of all young people, believers and non-believers alike. We must not make distinctions that lead to precluding dialogue: When I say all, I mean all. Are you young? You can talk; we're here to listen to you. There is a chance that before the Synod there will also be an assembly of young people, where they will be able to discuss different topics with one another and then bring their results to the bishops: I think that is the proper spirit to stimulate dialogue and positive conversation.

I have heard you speak often of the concept of craftsmanship. What does it mean for a young person to rediscover craftsmanship?

＝＝＝

IT MEANS REDISCOVERING "making," and here it has to do with industriousness. "Making" is creation and it is *poiesis,* that is, poetry. Craftsmanship is work and poetry . . . You are creative with your hands, with your heart, with your mind. This gives you spontaneity, the beauty of being yourself without overplanning every detail.

Think about soccer, a sport much loved by young

people all over the world: Nowadays it is even enjoyed in the United States, where previously the focus was mainly on American football. I think that the best soccer matches are the ones that spring up in the piazza: We just go "eenie, meenie, miney, mo" and see who'll be on the team. We'll pick up a couple of sticks from the ground and start building a gate, pretending that there is a net behind it. Then we'll decide who will be the goalkeeper, the famous "flying goalie," remember?

Yes, the player who can also leave the gate and score. The "flying goalie" is used when there are only a few players, did that happen to you, too?

———

SURE, YOU SEE? It takes very little to smile. We can smile about it because we are talking about soccer on an amateur level, not as business; we are thinking of soccer as enjoyment, as a reason to be together, united and only temporarily adversaries. Rediscovering craftsmanship means rediscovering amateurism. And being proud of doing so.

I would like to end by asking you this: What are the attributes that a young person should never lack?

———

PASSION AND JOY. And from there one can move on to talk about another quality that should not be lacking: a sense of humor. Related to an ability to take delight, to be enthusiastic, a sense of humor is essential in order to breathe. Humor also helps us to be in a good mood, and if we are in a good mood it is easier to get along with others and with ourselves.

Humor is like water that naturally flows, bubbling, from the spring. It has something more: You sense its life, its charge.

The English writer G. K. Chesterton wrote a very exemplary phrase about it: "Life is much too serious to be taken seriously."

Every day, for nearly forty years, I have asked the Lord for this blessing and I do it with a prayer written by Saint Thomas More. It is called "A Prayer for Good Humor" and reads as follows:

Grant me, O Lord, good digestion,
and also something to digest.

Grant me a healthy body,
and the necessary good humor to maintain it.

Grant me a simple soul
that knows to treasure all that is good

and that doesn't frighten easily at the sight of evil,
but rather finds
the means to put things back in their place.

Give me a soul that knows not boredom,
grumblings, sighs, and laments,
nor excess of stress, because of
that obstructing thing
called "I."

Grant me, O Lord, a sense of good humor.
Allow me the grace to be able to take a joke
to discover in life a bit of joy,
and to be able to share it with others.
† Amen.

Saint Thomas More is a figure I feel truly connected to. To understand what a courageous man he was, brimming with a sense of humor, just think about his final words: "This did not offend the king," he said, moving his beard aside so that it would not be nicked during his decapitation.

Returning to your question: First come passion and joy, next a sense of humor, and then harmony. Everything comes from harmony. Thanks to harmony we can be credible, and if we are credible we can be loved for what we really are, with no need of masks. After that comes fruitfulness: giving life to others. And I mean this term in a broad sense, not just being parents, although that is very important. I also mean a spiritual, cultural fecundity. It is very important that life include fecundity: We must be open to change and to others' viewpoints. We need the thoughts and perspectives of others, especially when they tell us something different, something new to us. To all young people, though not only to them, I say: Do not be afraid of the differences of others or your weaknesses; life is one of a kind and unique for what it is; God awaits us every morning when we wake up to once again give us this gift. Let us cherish it with love, kindness, and spontaneity.

ABOUT THE AUTHORS

JORGE MARIO BERGOGLIO was born in Buenos Aires on December 17, 1936. On March 13, 2013, he became the Bishop of Rome and the 266th Pope of the Catholic Church.

Twitter: @Pontifex

THOMAS LEONCINI was born in 1985 in La Spezia (Italy). A journalist and writer engaged in the study of psychological and social models, he is the co-author, with Zygmunt Bauman, of *Born Liquid* (Polity Press), which has been translated into twelve languages, and with Pope Francis of *Dio è giovane* (Piemme), released worldwide on March 20, 2018. His most recent collaborations as a journalist have been published in, among others, *Süddeutsche Zeitung, Folha de S.Paulo,* and *Znak.* His work has been mentioned in *El Mundo, El País, Le Figaro, Le Monde, Die Zeit, Frankfurter Allgemeine,* and *O Globo,* among others.

Facebook.com/thleoncini
Twitter: @thleoncini

ABOUT THE TRANSLATOR

ANNE MILANO APPEL has translated works by Claudio Magris, Paolo Giordano, Paolo Maurensig, Giuseppe Catozzella, Primo Levi, Roberto Saviano, and many others. Her awards include the Italian Prose in Translation Award (2015), the John Florio Prize for Italian translation (2013), and the Northern California Book Award for Translation (2014 and 2013).

amilanoappel.com
Twitter: @annemilanoappel